snail

Spot's Big Book of Words

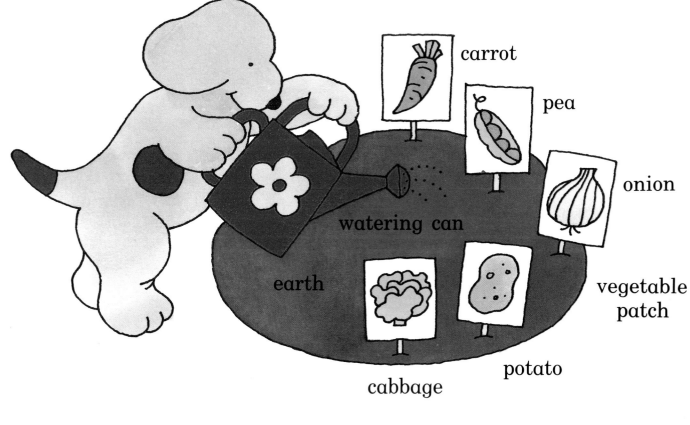

carrot

pea

onion

watering can

vegetable patch

earth

potato

cabbage

Eric Hill

freezer

✳ ✳ ✳

magnets

jug

orange juice

refrigerator

It's breakfast time and Spot gets the orange juice from the refrigerator. Sally is making cheese sandwiches for Sam.

cereal

milk jug

bowl

mug

kettle

coffee pot

toast

coffee

spoon

toaster

recorder

William Heinemann Limited
Michelin House, 81 Fulham Road, London SW3 6RB

LONDON MELBOURNE AUCKLAND

A Ventura book

First published 1988
© 1988 text and illustrations Eric Hill
Planned and produced by Ventura Publishing Limited
11-13 Young Street, Kensington, London W8 5EH
All rights reserved. First impression
434 94278 2

Printed and bound in Singapore by Tien Wah Press (Pte) Ltd.

curtains

window

sieve

saucepan

frying-pan

THE NEWS

teapot

plate

honey

knife

fork

eggs

tablecloth

bread knife

stove

cheese

bread

ring

mustard

sandwich

margarine

chimney

roof

farmhouse

sheep

fields

orchard

goose

fence

truck

Spot is helping his dad
on the farm. Tom and Helen
came along to help, but playing
with the wheelbarrow
is more fun.

wheelbarrow

horn

pond

duck

rope

ducklings

stake

hoof

frog

weather vane

dove

horseshoe

horse

barn

mouse

hay

stable

wheel

trailer

tractor

cow

cat

chicken

tail

cockerel

milk
bucket

milk churn

pig

clock

blackboard

chalk

teacher

book

bookcase

Spot is at school.
Tom is colouring a picture
with crayons and Spot
and Helen are painting
pictures on their easels.
Soon they will all go
outside to play.

building
bricks

ruler

glue

scissors

pencil

rubber

desk

workbook

satchel

crayons

bell

map

swing

slide

see-saw

playground

door

lunch box

thermos

tap

sink

easel

paper

brush

drip

apron

water jar

red

green

paint box

drawing pin

blue

yellow

keyboard

piano

Miss Bear's class is having a music lesson.
Spot thinks it's all great fun – what a noise they're making!

note

guitar

bow

violin

sheet music

harmonica

music stand

triangle

recorder

tambourine

Next door, Helen and Betsy are having a dance lesson. The teacher is going to play some ballet music on the stereo.

record

stereo

stereo speaker

Swan Lake

record cover

stage

steps

star

wand

spotlight

barre

tutu

wings

fairy costume

ballet shoes

cassette player

tape

Tom is painting the shed while Spot waters the vegetable seeds he has planted. Helen has picked some flowers to take home to her mother.

wall

hedge

gate

bush

path

apple tree

worm

leaf

buttercup

apple

butterfly

lawn

flowers

birdbath

flower bed

basket

seagull

rod

Spot is at the beach
and can't wait to get
to the sea! Helen, Steve
and Tom are at the beach, too.
What is Helen looking at
through her telescope?

aeroplan

float

line

pier

hook

seaweed

yacht

waves

fish

hat

surf

telescope

rubber
ring

bucket

steps

anchor

pebbles

suntan lotion

beach bag

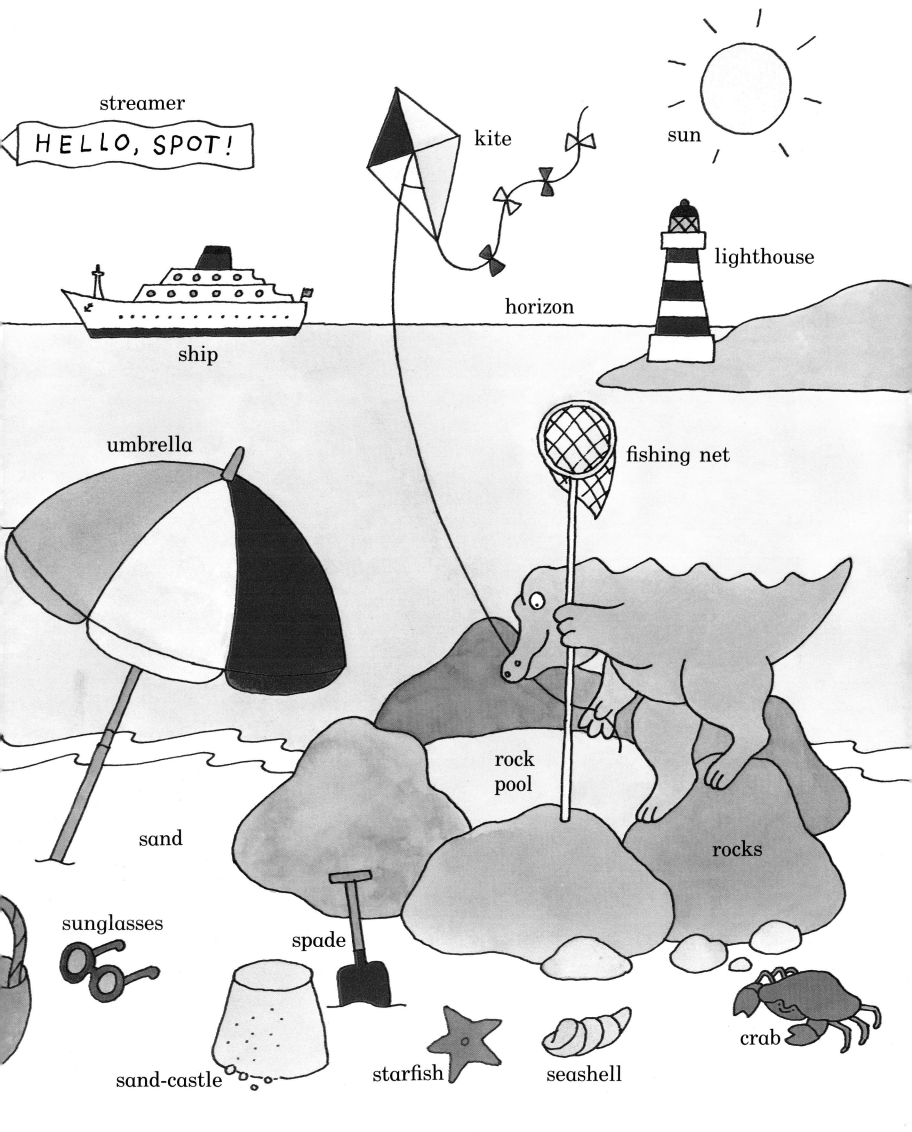

streamer

HELLO, SPOT!

kite

sun

lighthouse

horizon

ship

umbrella

fishing net

rock
pool

sand

rocks

sunglasses

spade

crab

sand-castle

starfish

seashell

plant

front door

feather
duster

grandfather
clock

chair

dust

broom

staircase

magazine

sofa

cushion

newspaper

It's house-cleaning time and Spot and his friends are helping Sally. Turn off the television, Steve!

mirror

tulips

light switch

curtain

television

telephone

vase

remote control

drawer

lampshade

chest

footstool

rug

table lamp

vacuum cleaner

coffee table

furniture wax

fruit bowl

It's such a fine day! Everyone is out in the park. Look at Tom on his new bicycle!

tennis ball

sun visor

tennis racket

net

roller skates

skipping rope

cap

hand brake

handlebars

pedal

tyre

bicycle

helmet

elbow pad

knee pad

skateboard

trampoline

headband

earphone

stopwatch

transistor
radio

jogging suit

sock

sole

jogging shoes

heel

tricycle

It's Spot's birthday and he has invited his friends to a birthday party. How old do you think Spot is today?
Count the candles on the cake!

Happy bi...

party hat

horn

ice cream

sandwiches

biscuits

sailing boat

lid

box

teddy bear

aeroplane

wardrobe

hanger

cupboard

belts

rail

jacket

skirt

blouse

T-shirt

shoes

party dress

jeans

mirror

handbag

drawer

beads

flip-flop

dress

Helen's mother has
bought a new dress and
sweater for Helen.
Do you like pink?
Helen does!

box

sweater

cowboy boot

cap

jacket

overalls

tie

shorts

trousers

duffel bag

moccasins

socks

rugby shirt

shirt

rain hat

boots

suitcase

trainers

umbrella

swimming trunks

Spot is helping Steve pack for a holiday. Steve can't find a pair of socks that match. Look under the drawer, Steve!

ski poles

goggles

Spot and his friends are
enjoying some winter fun.
Helen made the snowman
and his dog. Spot thinks
the dog looks like him!

ski boots

skis

mountains

fur hat

snowball

earmuffs

frozen pond

broom

pipe

ice skates

mittens

snowman

scarf

boots

snowdog

snow

chimney

smoke

fir tree

icicle

log cabin

woolly hat

snowflake

gloves

sledge

robin

footprints

log

Spot is staying overnight
at Tom's house.
Tom wants Spot to share the
bunk bed, but Spot pretends
he is camping out in his
sleeping bag.
Sleep well, Spot!

calendar

MAY
S M T W T F S
1 2 3 4 5 6 7
8 9 10 11 12 13 14
15 16 17 18 19 20 21
22 23 24 25 26 27 28
29 30 31

pyjamas

pinboard

clock

bedside table

sheet

blanket

slippers

bunk bed

ladder

pillow

shower curtain

cabinet

hook

toothbrush

shower

bath toy

toothpaste

shower cap

sponge

soap

tap

radio

toilet paper

sink

towel

bath

toilet

dressing gown

bath mat

sleeping bag

zip

torch

rucksack

biscuits